Burmese Pythons Invade the Everglades

By Susan H. Gray

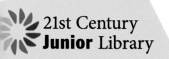
21st Century
Junior Library

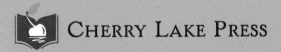
CHERRY LAKE PRESS

Published in the United States of America by Cherry Lake Publishing Group
Ann Arbor, Michigan
www.cherrylakepublishing.com

Reading Adviser: Beth Walker Gambro, MS, Ed., Reading Consultant, Yorkville, IL
Book Designer: Melinda Millward

Photo Credits: © Heiko Kiera/Shutterstock.com, cover; © CGN089/Shutterstock.com, 4;
© Heiko Kiera/Shutterstock.com, 6, 8; © bluedogstudio/Shutterstock.com, 10; © Thomas Barrat/
Shutterstock.com, 12; © Utopia_88/iStock.com, 14; © Krasula/Shutterstock.com, 16; © dwi putra
stock/Shutterstock.com, 18; © Patrick K. Campbell/Shutterstock.com, 20

Cherry Lake Press is an imprint of Cherry Lake Publishing Group.

Library of Congress Cataloging-in-Publication Data

Names: Gray, Susan Heinrichs, author.
Title: Burmese pythons invade the Everglades / by Susan H. Gray.
Description: Ann Arbor, Michigan : Cherry Lake Publishing, 2021. | Series:
    Invasive species science : tracking and controlling | Includes index. | Audience: Grades 2-3
Identifiers: LCCN 2021004874 (print) | LCCN 2021004875 (ebook) | ISBN 9781534187023
    (hardcover) | ISBN 9781534188426 (paperback) | ISBN 9781534189829 (pdf) | ISBN
    9781534191228 (ebook)
Subjects: LCSH: Burmese python—Control—Florida—Everglades—Juvenile literature. |
    Introduced reptiles—Florida—Everglades—Juvenile literature. | Invasive species—
    Control—Florida—Everglades—Juvenile literature.
Classification: LCC QL666.O63 G735 2021 (print) | LCC QL666.O63 (ebook) |
    DDC 597.96/780975939—dc23
LC record available at https://lccn.loc.gov/2021004874
LC ebook record available at https://lccn.loc.gov/2021004875

Cherry Lake Publishing Group would like to acknowledge the work of the Partnership for 21st
Century Learning, a Network of Battelle for Kids. Please visit http://www.battelleforkids.org/
networks/p21 for more information.

Printed in the United States of America
Corporate Graphics

CONTENTS

5 A Creepy Scene

9 Plenty of Pythons

13 Some Early Efforts

19 Cold, Dead Snakes

22 Glossary

23 Find Out More

24 Index

24 About the Author

The Burmese python is one of the largest snakes.

A Creepy Scene

"Hey! Let's put him over there!" It was nighttime in **rural** Florida. Two men hopped out of a pickup. A large ice chest sat in the truck bed. One man popped it open. Coiled inside was a **Burmese python**—dead and still cold from being kept in a freezer. Together, the men pulled the **reptile** from its cooler.

Burmese pythons are hard to spot. They **camouflage** into the environment.

The python's coils loosened a bit, and its body sagged. One man lugged it to the roadside and placed it where the other had pointed. Meanwhile, their fellow scientists and engineers climbed from their vehicles. The researchers were there to photograph the **invasive** Burmese python.

Ask Questions!

Burmese pythons normally live in Myanmar, which was once called Burma, and other nearby countries. But now they also live in Florida. Find Myanmar on a map. How is it similar to Florida? Why would pythons do well in Florida?

The Burmese python is a threat to wildlife in southern Florida. They can hide in the water or on land.

Plenty of Pythons

Burmese pythons normally live in southern Asia. They probably came to the United States as part of the **exotic** pet trade.

Think!

The exotic pet trade continues. How would you convince a friend not to get an exotic pet?

A Burmese python's eggs hatch in 2 to 3 months.

In the 1970s, python owners in Florida began releasing their pets. Pythons freed in the **Everglades** were lucky. The area is warm and wet and offers plenty of **prey**. Pythons mated and females laid eggs—40, 50, or 60 at a time. Before long, there were thousands of pythons.

Prey animals were disappearing. Raccoon, bobcat, and fox populations have shrunk dramatically. Marsh rabbits are completely gone.

Signs were posted in parks and along waterways.

Some Early Efforts

Pythons were wrecking the **food web** in the Everglades. The government asked volunteers to hunt the pythons. Some people used dogs to track them.

Look!

Find some photos of other snakes. Look at the colors and patterns on their skin. Which ones have camouflage similar to the python?

The number of pythons caught tripled after 2017.

Nothing worked. At best, only a few hundred snakes were killed each year.

In 2017, wildlife experts started a new program. They paid people to hunt the snakes. In 2020, the experts held the first-ever Python Bowl. It was a 10-day hunt for pythons. More than 700 people from 20 states came. Together, they removed 80 snakes from south Florida.

Make a Guess!

One goal of the Python Bowl was to raise awareness of the pythons. Why is it important to educate people about invasive **species?**

Different types of cameras have been used
to track many different species.

The problem with hunting is that it takes a lot of time. Scientists in Florida are working on new cameras that could speed up the search.

The cameras see beyond what the human eye can see. They see light waves that people cannot. A python's skin reflects a whole range of light waves. Humans can see enough to know they are looking at a python. But the cameras see more. They can see the python's skin reflecting light waves even when the snake is hidden by plants.

Young Burmese pythons will spend time in trees.

Cold, Dead Snakes

These Florida scientists tested their cameras. To be safe, they used dead snakes. The snakes were kept cold so they wouldn't **decay**. The scientists placed their snakes in different areas, including ponds and roadsides.

On camera, the snakes almost glowed. Even when surrounded by leaves, grass, and weeds, their images were easy to spot.

Now, no one knows how many pythons are in south Florida.
Most estimates are more than 100,000.

The scientists believe that their cameras could help hunters spot pythons quickly. Cameras might be mounted on truck rooftops. Passengers could watch a screen for signs of the invaders. Hunters can carry a hand-held camera around a pond. The pythons would be up against new technology. Even the best camouflage wouldn't help them. Perhaps soon, there will be a solution to Florida's python problem.

GLOSSARY

Burmese (buhr-MEEZ) coming from or living in Burma

camouflage (KAM-uh-flahzh) a means of hiding by using patterns, colors, or markings

decay (di-KAY) to rot or break down

Everglades (EH-vur-glaydz) a large, swampy area in southern Florida

exotic (eg-ZOT-ik) coming from a foreign land; very unusual

food web (FOOD WEB) the network of what eats what in a community

invasive (in-VAY-sihv) not native, but entering by force or by accident and spreading quickly

prey (PRAY) animals that are hunted and eaten by other animals

python (PY-thon) a large snake that kills its prey by coiling tightly around it

reptile (REP-tile) a cold-blooded animal such as a turtle, lizard, or snake

rural (ROOR-uhl) out in the country; not in town

species (SPEE-sheez) a particular kind of plant or animal

FIND OUT MORE

BOOKS

Ciletti, Barbara J. *Burmese Pythons*. Mankato, MN: Black Rabbit Books, 2017.

Gilles, Renae. *Invasive Species in Infographics*. Ann Arbor, MI: Cherry Lake Publishing, 2020.

Oachs, Emily Rose. *Burmese Pythons*. Minneapolis, MN: Bellwether Media, 2014.

WEBSITES

DK Findout!—Snakes
https://www.dkfindout.com/us/animals-and-nature/reptiles/snakes
Discover some amazing facts about snakes and link to a few of the different snake groups.

National Geographic Kids—Super Snakes
https://kids.nationalgeographic.com/explore/nature/super-snakes
Learn some amazing things about how snakes see, hear, smell, and find their food.

San Diego Zoo Kids—Python
https://kids.sandiegozoo.org/animals/python
Find plenty of information and great photos here.

INDEX

Burmese pythons
    camouflage, 6, 21
    eggs, 10, 11
    food, 11, 13
    hunting, 13, 14, 15, 17
    as invasive species, 7
    numbers in Florida, 20
    as pets, 9, 11
    prey, 11
    released into the Everglades, 11
    size, 4
    skin, 17
    as threat to wildlife, 8
    tracking, 16, 17, 19, 21
    where they live, 7, 9, 18

cameras, 16, 17, 19, 21
camouflage, 6, 21

eggs, 10, 11
Everglades, 11, 13. *See also* Florida
exotic pets, 9, 11

Florida, 5, 7, 8, 11, 20. *See also* Everglades
food, 11
food web, 13

hunting, 13, 14, 15, 17

invasive species, 7, 15

pets, 9, 11
prey, 11
Python Bowl, 15

reptile, 5

skin, 17

tracking, 16, 17, 19, 21

ABOUT THE AUTHOR

Susan H. Gray has a master's degree in zoology. She has written more than 180 reference books for children and especially loves writing about animals. Susan lives in Cabot, Arkansas, with her husband, Michael, and many pets.